W9-DCN-076

10! Marshall Ramsey's TEN-YEAR CELEBRATION

The best editorial cartoons from Marshall Ramsey's first decade at *The Clarion-Ledger*
Katrina • Electionman the Next Generation • The Cowboy • Pulitzer cartoons • and more

The Clarion-Ledger
clarionledger.com ■ REAL MISSISSIPPI

Visit Marshall Ramsey's blog at www.clarionledger.com/ramsey

DEDICATION

To my family:
The one at home, the one at *The Clarion-Ledger* and the one at Copley News Service.
Without you, this would be a book of blank paper.

Back cover photo by **Barbara Gauntt** • Cover illustration and graphic design by **Marshall Ramsey** • Edited by **Joe White**

Copyright © 2006 *The Clarion-Ledger*

All rights reserved. No part of this book may be reproduced, stored in a retrieval system or transmitted in any form or by any means, electronic, mechanical, photocopying, recording or otherwise, without prior written permission of the copyright owner or the publisher.

Published for *The Clarion-Ledger* by Pediment Publishing, a division of The Pediment Group, Inc. • www.pediment.com
ISBN 1-59725-072-4

Marshall Ramsey's cartoons are distributed nationally by Copley News Service. For more information, call 800-238-6196

Other books written or illustrated by Marshall Ramsey:
Marshall Ramsey's Greatest Hits by Marshall Ramsey, *Nobody's Poet* by Robert St. John,.
The Life Lessons with Junior Series by Dave Ramsey: *The Super Red Racer - Junior Discovers Work*,
My Fantastic Field trip - Junior Discovers Saving, *The Big Birthday Surprise - Junior Discovers Giving*,
Careless at the Carnival - Junior Discover Spending, *A Special Thank You - Junior Discovers Integrity*
and *Battle of the Chores - Junior Discovers Debt*.

Foreword

A good laugh is the best way to start most days. A dear friend encouraged me to go straight to B.C., or one of the other comic strips, first thing in the morning to start my day.

Little did I know, these days, my morning laugh would be aimed at my husband. Instead of going to the comic strips, I go straight to the editorial section of *The Clarion-Ledger*. Readers may be surprised how often I laugh out loud as Marshall Ramsey makes Haley his target.

Marshall is not mean or a cheap-shot artist. He has a rapier-like wit and is a clever, talented caricaturist. He's not labeled a conservative, liberal, Republican or Democrat; he is an equal opportunity abuser. Marshall demonstrates a wise grasp of the public policy issues and has a feel for the politicians who have to grapple with them.

Wow! Does he have a keen eye, or what? You know, Haley and I have been married for thirty-five years, and I never noticed the gap between his front teeth! I would say it's wide enough to park a FEMA trailer!

Mississippians are blessed to have a cartoonist at our largest newspaper who is one of the best in his profession. Marshall has been nominated twice for a Pulitzer Prize, and we, his admirers, know it's only a matter of time before he is properly recognized.

Marsha Barbour
First Lady of Mississippi

Following Hurricane Katrina in August of 2005, Marsha Barbour spent 70 of the first 90 days on the Mississippi Gulf Coast helping the victims of the storm.

Greetings from a cartoonist's paradise: Mississippi

© 1996 THE CLARION-LEDGER

I haven't crammed this much since my ninth-grade World History final exam.

Except, this time I wasn't shoving facts about Constantine into my head. I was stuffing cartoons into this book. Picking from over 3,600 cartoons to fill 140 spots, to be exact.

It was like trying to fit the old Elvis into a Speedo.

Any one of the book's sections could have had its own book. For example, I had 153 Frank Melton cartoons to choose from. I have at least that many Katrina cartoons. And I could do a book on state politics thicker than the London phone book.

Deciding what made the cut was hard – I know I left out someone's favorite cartoon. Please allow me to me to apologize in advance. I just picked the best way I that knew how: These are cartoons that I really like. Originally, this was supposed to be a sequel to my first book, *Marshall Ramsey's Greatest Hits*. But recently, I discovered a box filled with my very first cartoons that didn't make the last book. So, with my 10th anniversary at *The Clarion-Ledger* coming up, I expanded the book's focus. And ran out of room very

My first cartoon that appeared in *The Clarion-Ledger*. It was printed on December 17, 1996. If I had really spilled that much ink, I would have been fired.

quickly. If you want to see more cartoons, buy lots of this book so there'll be another one. I'm starting by buying

Continued on the next page

two for my friend Dan Turner.

Who's Dan Turner, you ask?

Well, if you like my cartoons, he's the one you should thank. It was his phone call that got me here ten years ago. I was in San Diego, California soaking up the sun and losing my Southern accent. And then the phone rang.

Funny how a single phone call can change your life.

Dan was my editor when I worked in Conroe, Texas, a small town outside of Houston. He's also a native of Philadelphia, Mississippi, who just happened to be in Jackson that day. He called to let me know that there was an opening at *The Clarion-Ledger*. He said I would love the job.

Dan, you were right.

This *is* my dream job.

The last ten years have been one blessing after another. I work with amazingly talented people. My editor David Hampton is not only wise but he pushes me to be better. I couldn't ask for more from an editor. The other people in my department, Jim Ewing, Joe White and Sid Salter, have, if you will pardon the cliché, forgotten more about Mississippi than most people will ever know. And, they are all extremely funny. Our morning meetings produce more laughter than most stand-up routines. I credit them with much of my professional success.

Mississippi is the best place in the world to be an editorial cartoonist.

I've also had a string of good publishers and executive editors who have allowed me the professional freedom to do what I do. That is invaluable. I want to thank John Newhouse and Ronnie Agnew, my current publisher and executive editor for greenlighting this book's publication.

I've also been blessed personally. My wife and I now have two small, genuine Mississippians running around the house. And five years, ago, I received another blessing – I survived malignant melanoma. I want to take a second to thank Dr. Ken Barraza for saving my life. There would be no ten-year collection if it weren't for him.

Mississippi is the best place in the world to be an editorial cartoonist. And I hope this book proves it. This is a ten-year slice of history from my eyes. I've seen three very different governors, senators who rose and fell out of national prominence, a daily parade of humor come out of Jackson – both from City Hall and the Capitol, a man-made disaster (WorldCom) and a natural one (Katrina.) But what has been consistent is obvious: the kindness and strength of the people of Mississippi.

I want to thank everyone in the state for the support of my work — you've made this a ten-year celebration indeed.

Hurricane Katrina and the recovery

I was coming back from a book signing in Memphis late on a Saturday night. As my car headed south on I-55, I noticed something I had never seen before — cars. Lots of cars. Usually driving through Holmes County at 10:30 at night is like driving through ink. But that night was different. There was a string of headlights that extended as far as I could see. It looked like the end of the movie *Field of Dreams*.

That's when Katrina first came onto my radar.

I immediately turned on WWL out of New Orleans and heard the pleas for everyone to get out. They were the most dire warnings I had ever heard. At that moment, I knew it was going to be bad.

But I couldn't have imagined how bad it turned out to be. And how bad it would still be a year later.

I am proud of these cartoons — not because I think they are some kind of masterpieces — but because of the e-mails, letters and calls I received because of them. They made a difference in the lives of people who Katrina directly affected. And for me, that is better than a thousand Pulitzers.

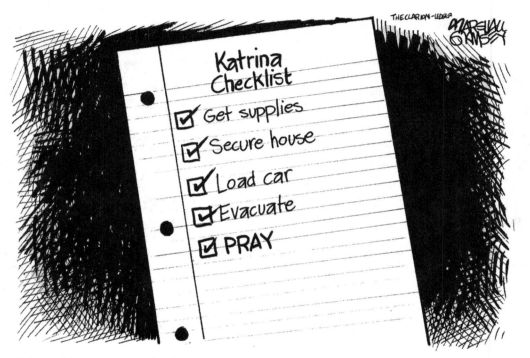

I drew this cartoon on the Sunday before the storm. By then, I think we knew that Katrina could approach Camille in destruction. It turned out to be much worse.

This is a story that just won't go away overnight. Replacing the housing lost on the Mississippi Gulf Coast will take over a decade. So when I do my 20th anniversary book, I'm 100% sure there will be Katrina cartoons in it, too.

STORM SURGE

The Clarion-Ledger
COPLEY NEWS SERVICE

DISASTER RELIEF

In Jackson, we couldn't see the forest for the trees — the trees that had taken out the power lines. So, it was a couple of days before I saw the first images from the Coast. The Biloxi Lighthouse was the first landmark I recognized.

2006 Pulitzer Finalist

BIRD of PRAY

2006 Pulitzer Finalist

The Clarion-Ledger
COPLEY NEWS SERVICE

JOHN GRISHAM

GULF COAST

$5 MILLION GIFT

A TIME TO GIVE

"☆☆☆☆☆ AN EXAMPLE FOR ALL OF US"
— Mississippi Residents

The Clarion-Ledger
COPLEY NEWS SERVICE
MARSHALL RAMSEY

2006
Pulitzer
Finalist

The heroes of the storm. When the power was restored, so was hope. This cartoon was reprinted by several power companies and handed out to the workers who came down to help. This is my favorite cartoon from the storm.

With most of the national media attention focused on the disaster in New Orleans, the Gulf Coast and particularly inland areas were virtually ignored. Being nationally syndicated has its benefits.

2006 Pulitzer Finalist

2006
Pulitzer
Finalist

Michael Brown was made a scapegoat — but it still was good to see him go. Heckuva job, Brownie. Don't let the door hit you on the way out.

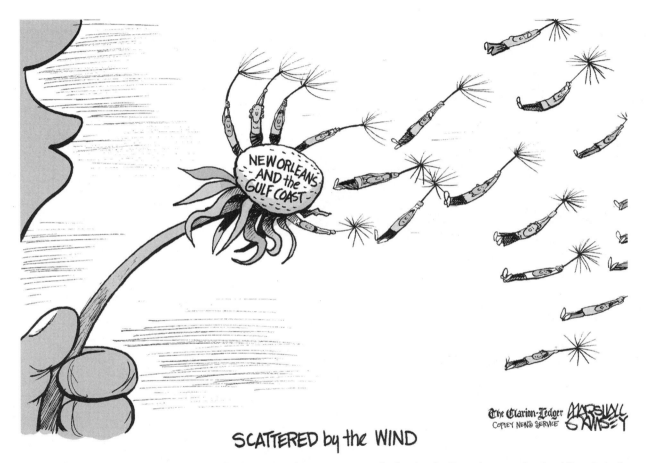

SCATTERED by the WIND

The Clarion-Ledger
COPLEY NEWS SERVICE

MARSHALL RAMSEY

It was the biggest migration since the Dust Bowl. I met a couple in the Dallas airport who had lived their whole lives in New Orleans. They had lost their home and business — and were starting a new life in Amarillo.

2006
Pulitzer
Finalist

EARL FINALLY FINDS A USE FOR ALL of the HURRICANE-RELATED PAPERWORK HE HAS HAD to FILL OUT.

TROPICAL DEPRESSION

2006
Pulitzer
Finalist

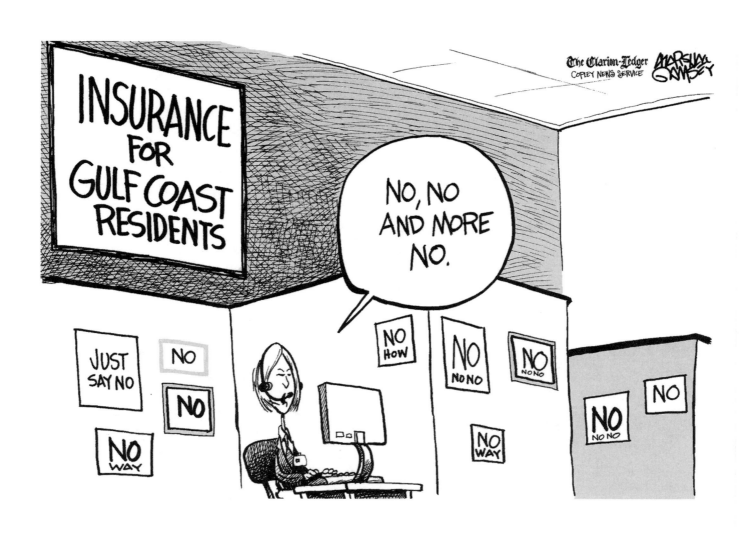

THIS IS A
FEMA TRAILER

SODA

THIS IS A
HURRICANE.
ANY QUESTIONS?

RAIL CROSS

WIND versus WATER

A.G. HOOD

LAWSUIT

INSURANCE COMMISSIONER DALE

2-4-6-8 Let's all Mediate

The Clarion-Ledger

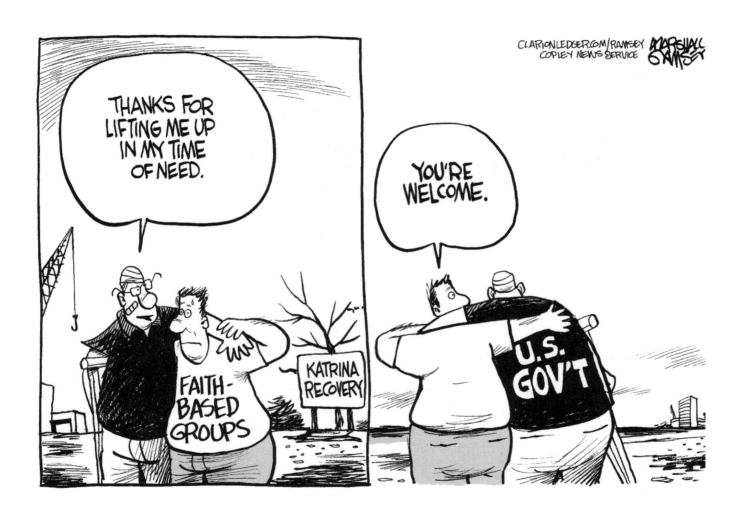

The next four images are drawings I did while on an early December work trip at Camp Coast Care in Long Beach. This is in Pass Christian looking south toward the water. Six people died in this scene.

One of my favorite places in Mississippi was the bike path along the beachfront in Bay St. Louis and Waveland. This is in Waveland looking east toward Bay St. Louis. The million-dollar mansions are now history.

Battered American flags were symbolic of the battered Americans who hung them. When I drew this, Congress was trying to back away from some of its promises of relief. The irony was as thick as the debris.

This is a home we cleared in Waveland. It had survived
Camille.

Ancient history: My first cartoons

It's tough following someone who has been in your job for years. I knew coming into this job that *The Clarion-Ledger* had a long tradition of good editorial cartoonists. Filling my predecessor's shoes wouldn't be easy.

A few months ago, I had to dig out a pre-2000 original editorial cartoon for an art exhibit in England. I never did find it (I think it is at Mississippi State Library where some of my early cartoons are), but I did find a lot of cartoons that I hadn't seen in years. It was like a reunion.

I had forgotten that I had drawn Lucky Dupree. And I wondered why I had a jar of Grey Poupon on my desk. And I found the first cartoon I ever had reprinted in *Newsweek* turning yellow in the bottom of a box. I will have to get it framed.

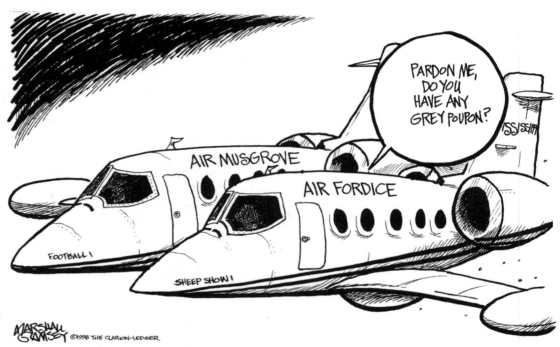

Lt. Gov. Ronnie Musgrove and Gov. Kirk Fordice were wearing out the state plane. Musgrove sent over a gift-wrapped jar of Grey Poupon the day after this cartoon ran.

Here are some of my favorites of the old stuff. It's interesting to see how my work has evolved. Notice how my lettering has changed. And you can see how some of the local characters also have changed over time. Mike Moore's hair was shorter. Kirk Fordice didn't have a beret. Plus, Kane Ditto even makes an appearance.

I don't know if I ever filled any shoes. I probably haven't even filled a sandal. But I've had a fun time trying.

"I THOUGHT I WAS O.K. 'CAUSE THE AGE OF CONSENT IN MISSISSIPPI IS 14... BUT THEN I GAVE HER A CIGARETTE."

I saw a yellowed copy of this at a store recently. The age of consent has risen to 16. Why don't I feel better?

Everyone's platform was to blame Kane Ditto for everything. Note the early Harvey Johnson caricature.

People ask me if I have ever regretted drawing a cartoon. To be honest, no. But this cartoon comes close. I think the tone is wrong. When you first move into a town, you are tone deaf — it takes a while to get the nuances.

"AFTER WE STEAL YOUR LAND AND BREAK OUR TREATIES, WE'LL TAX YOUR CASINO."

CHRISTMAS EVE ON COUNTY LINE ROAD

My first cartoon in which I did upper-case letters in the word balloon. It is also my first cartoon in *Newsweek*.

Pre-diamond Kirk and short-haired Mike. Mike Moore complained about how tall his hair was after this cartoon. I made it taller, of course. And taller. And taller.

For example.

Electionman and the Cowboy ride again

Back in 2001, I created the comic strip Electionman. Electionman was about a mild-mannered mayor who became a superhero only during election time. Once a week, Electionman would take flight until eventually, both candidates started referring to themselves as their character's names (which scared me). That series was in my first book and was wildly popular.

Last year, Electionman took flight again against a new nemesis, the Cowboy. The Cowboy was a reckless former television executive who would say and do anything to get elected. He ran a terrible campaign and created the most unlikely coalition in the history of Jackson. He also won by a landslide.

After the first series, Electionman went away — because Harvey Johnson went back to his old, plodding and planning self. But Cowboy is still with us because Frank Melton does bizarre things on a daily basis. He has turned the six o'clock news into my strip. So I still draw him with his cowboy hat and pistols. And expect to get shot any day now.

Here's the second Electionman series and some of my favorite Frank Melton cartoons. (I could do a whole book on Frank alone.)

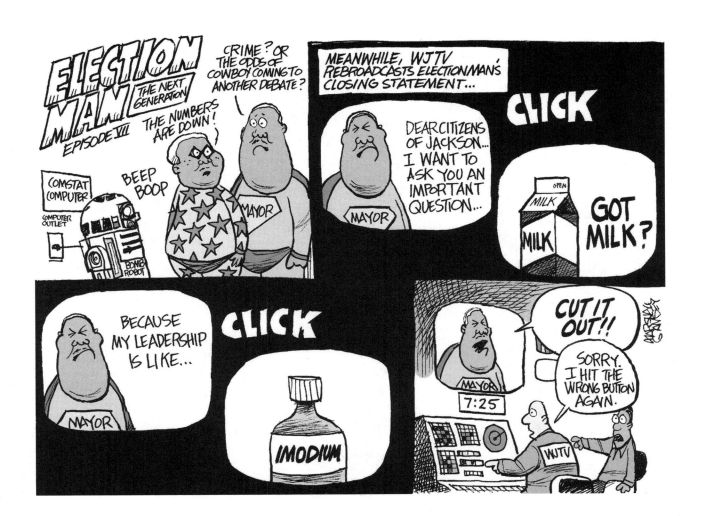

CLARIONLEDGER.COM/RAMSEY
COPLEY NEWS SERVICE
MARSHALL RAMSEY
Frank says so...
We the People
HUG
ME
PAINT
MUCH BETTER.

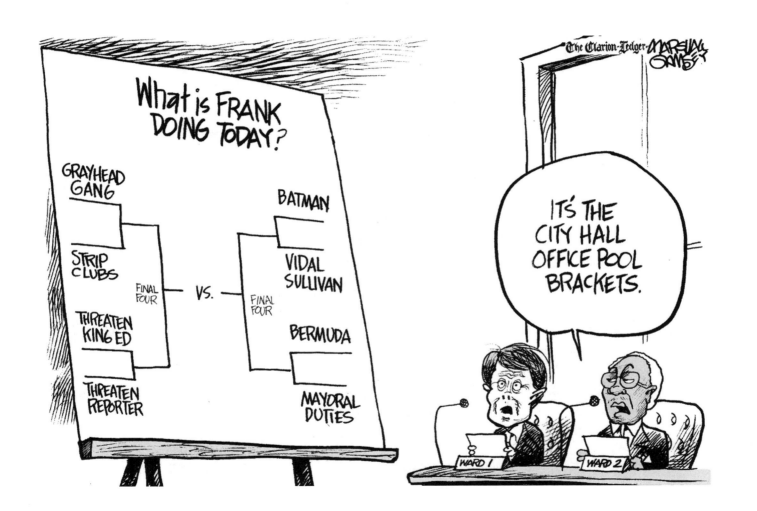

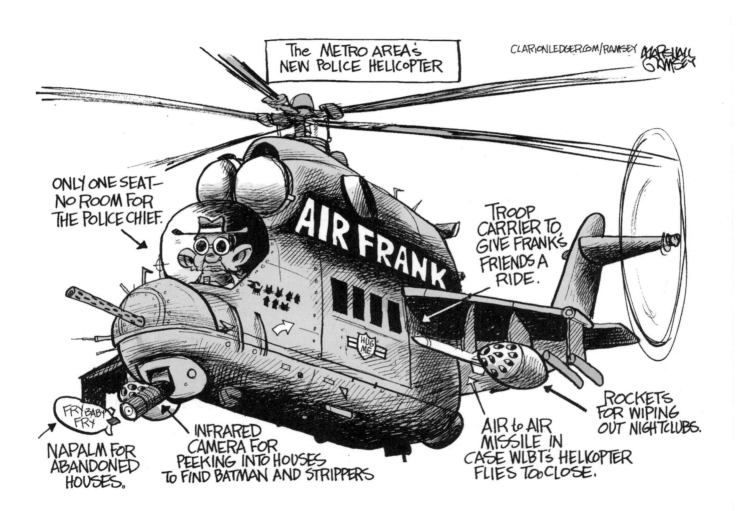

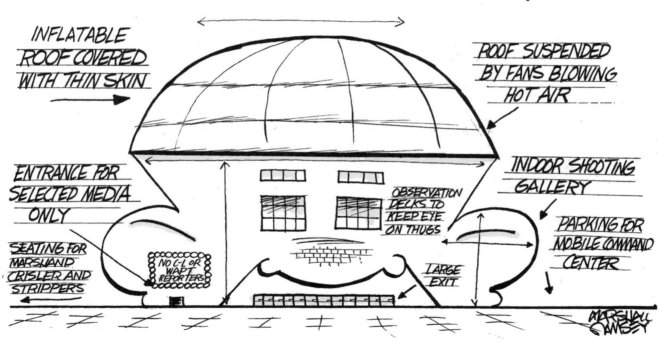

"You're only as good as your governor"

Chris Britt, an excellent editorial cartoonist in Springfield, Illinois, once told me, "You're only as good as your governor."

Ours make me look like a genius.

Gov. Kirk Fordice was a very smart man who couldn't survive in the political world. He was used to running his own business and telling other people what do to. He tried that with the Legislature, Mike Moore and anyone else within earshot. In the end, only Lance, his beloved dog, would obey his commands. Governor Fordice lost his battle to cancer a couple of years ago, and I have to admit, I miss the old guy.

Gov. Ronnie Musgrove was elected over Mike Parker by the House and promptly alienated them in about 35 seconds. He broke Governor Ray Mabus' record by a whole minute. Musgrove spent the next four years

I was once told that if Ronnie Musgrove's nose looked like I drew it, he would drown when he tried to drink out of a glass.

always trying the sell something. His biggest victory was the Nissan plant — he has the logo tattooed on his chest.

Governor Barbour is to politics to what Michael Jordan was to basketball. He makes it look easy. Although I don't always agree with his politics, I admire

his smoothness. He has made the governor's office powerful by controlling the Senate. And he plays chess while the House plays checkers — he constantly stays two moves ahead of lawmakers.

Here are some of my favorite guv cartoons.

At the last moment, I drew a beret on the governor like the one Monica wore. I wanted him to have a souvenir from Paris. The next day, more people were talking about the beret than the rest of the cartoon. I let him keep it.

I never could figure out what "Only Positive Mississippi Spoken Here" meant. But I know it wasn't "I'll whip your a**."
After that clip ran on the *Today* show, I got calls from cartoonists across the country telling me how lucky I was.

IS IT LIVE OR IS IT FORDICE?

DAY ONE OF FORDICE'S RETIREMENT

My second all-time favorite cartoon. The next day I got this cartoon with my picture on Bert Case's body. The caption read, "Day two of Fordice's Retirement."

I put this one in here because it is the best caricature of Musgrove I have ever drawn. I got his body language down perfect. Of course, it only took me six years to get it right.

Mitch Tyner, a trial lawyer, was running against Barbour and kept calling him a "fat cat." This is early Haley — I couldn't get him drawn correctly until I saw a box of Fruity Pebbles. Haley Barbour looks like Fred Flintstone!

I couldn't send him off in a sappy way — it just wasn't him. The Fordice family owns this original.

The fourth panel sent me to therapy. Some things, even if they are for comedic effect, should never be drawn.

Drawing here is like fishing in a stocked pond

People ask me, "Where do you get your ideas?" I usually joke that I have a crack team of comedy writers working at the Capitol. But to be honest, that isn't far from the truth. I usually only have to open up the paper and look at the front page to find my idea. It's like fishing in a stocked pond.

Here are a few of my favorite state cartoons from the past few years. The beef plant debacle kept me very busy — I drew so many cartoons on it that my cholesterol went up. The WorldCom disaster finally resulted in Bernie Ebbers being sentenced to prison. Edgar Ray Killen was convicted for his part in the Neshoba killings, allowing healing to finally begin to take place. Ole Miss thought about getting rid of Colonel Reb, but decided to ditch the football coach instead. The suburbs are still growing and the state budget is still broke. At least some things are constant.

We lost Sonny Montgomery — or I should say, the enlisted man lost him. U.S. Sen. Trent Lott tripped over his tongue and then was pushed down by Sen. Bill Frist. He is now presently on his comeback tour. And as of this writing, Amy Tuck is still a Republican. But that could change at any moment.

Like I said, it's too easy being a cartoonist here.

I did so many beef plant cartoons my cholesterol jumped 50 points. This one is my favorite of the bunch.

THE REVISED MISSISSIPPI QUARTER

Mary Hawkins Butler, the mayor of Madison, has a way of getting her way. Ask Walmart (actually, the store does look pretty darn nice for a Walmart.)

Chuck Espy took on Bennie Thompson for the 2nd Congressional seat. You will never guess who won.

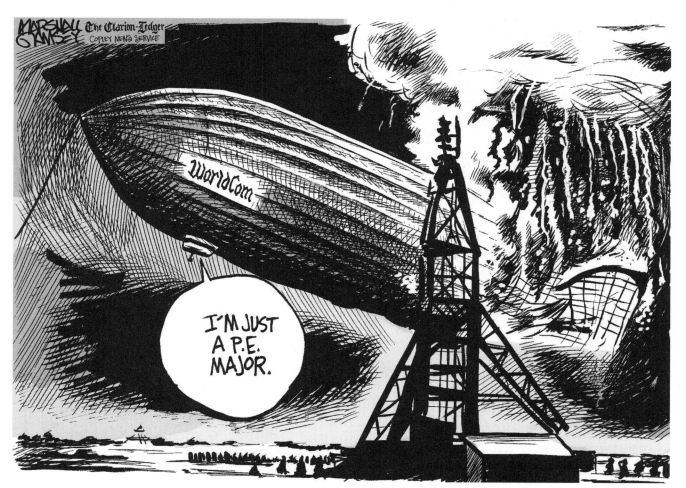

Bernie's famous quote from his trial. I should have used that one more myself.

Republican Amy Tuck took a loan from trial lawyer Dickie Scruggs. The irony was as sweet as the icing on a cake.

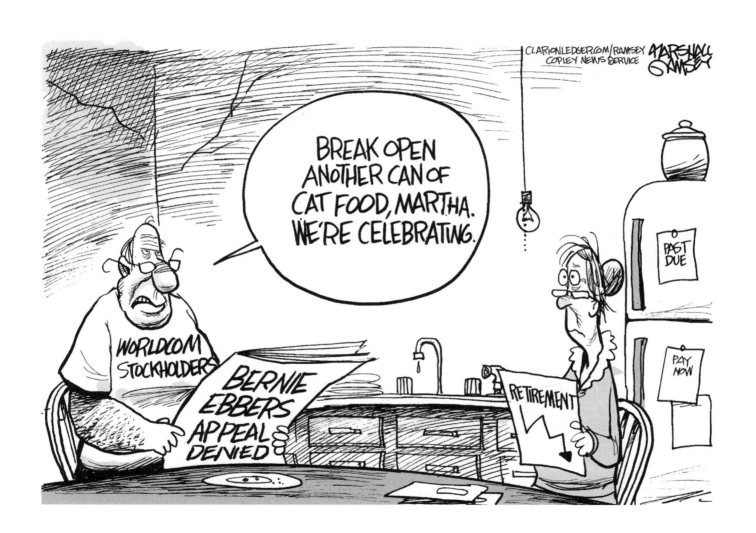

This is one of my favorite ideas ever.

House Speaker Bill McCoy's junker cars kept getting stolen from the motel parking lot.

Congressman Sonny Montgomery was an enlisted person's friend. He will be missed.

The Clarion-Ledger
COPLEY NEWS SERVICE
MARSHALL RAMSEY
Re-elect
TRENT LOTT
"I KNOW SOMETHING ABOUT RECOVERING FROM A DISASTER!"
CATCHY SLOGAN.
GULF COAST

TUCK, CHUCK, PUCK AND A LAME DUCK

JUSTICE IN
NESHOBA COUNTY

MARSHALL
RAMSEY
THE CLARION-LEDGER
COPLEY NEWS SERVICE

MISSISSIPPI BURNING

2006
Pulitzer
Finalist

EVOLUTION of the ROBE IN MISSISSIPPI

1964

2005

"JUSTICE"

MOB RULE

JUSTICE

LAW

The Clarion-Ledger
COPLEY NEWS SERVICE

MARSHALL RAMSEY

2006
Pulitzer
Finalist

On those days when there isn't a local cartoon

One of my favorite cartoons is in this section. It shows Lance Armstrong outpacing both the Tour de France (which he did seven times in a row) and cancer. It's special to me because I had cancer at the time I drew it — I am a malignant melanoma survivor. And the Lance Armstrong Foundation has used the cartoon on its website. So to think that I was able to help another cancer survivor is pretty cool to me.

But having cancer taught me one skill that is very very valuable these days: If you can laugh at what frightens you, you'll live a healthier and happier life. I guess I should have known that even before I had cancer; I do it for a living. But it's easier said than done.

I bring that up because we live in some fairly scary times. I try to laugh at the news, but stories like bird flu, terrorism, war, hurricanes, nuclear weapons in the hands of rogue states, etc. make it tough some days. But I try. And here are some of my cartoons since 9/11.

Even though most of the 9/11 cartoons were in the last book, I put my favorites in this one, too. The Eagle head

The Clarion-Ledger
COPLEY NEWS SERVICE

HAPPY VALENTINE'S DAY from DICK CHENEY

People had accused Dick Cheney of not being a straight shooter. We now know for sure. The joke went that Cheney shot the only lawyer in Texas who supported the Bush administration.

cartoon is my favorite all-time cartoon — I think its message still stands even today. Look what happened after Katrina. Even though our government was inept, we came together and helped out neighbors in need. United we stood.

UNITED WE STAND

2002 Pulitzer Finalist

The Clarion-Ledger
COPLEY NEWS SERVICE

The Clarion-Ledger
COPLEY NEWS SERVICE

AL GORE

POLITICAL CAREER

GLOBAL WARMING

ACE IN THE HOLE

NEXT ON LOST

POLLS

2006 Pulitzer Finalist

CHRISTOPHER REEVE

The Clarion-Ledger
COPLEY NEWS SERVICE